Out and About at the Supermarket

Stoneleigh Elementary School
Baltimore County Public Schools

By Kitty Shea
Illustrated by Becky Shipe

Special thanks to our advisers for their expertise:

Timothy Sperry, Director of Groceries, Northeast Region
Whole Foods Market

Susan Kesselring, M.A., Literacy Educator
Rosemount-Apple Valley-Eagan (Minnesota) School District

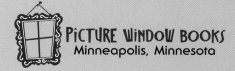

PICTURE WINDOW BOOKS
Minneapolis, Minnesota

The author wishes to thank Mike Conkey and Gary Larges
of Rick's Market, Navarre, Minnesota.

Managing Editor: Bob Temple
Creative Director: Terri Foley
Editor: Peggy Henrikson
Editorial Adviser: Andrea Cascardi
Copy Editor: Laurie Kahn
Designer: John Moldstad
Page production: Picture Window Books
The illustrations in this book were prepared digitally.

Picture Window Books
5115 Excelsior Boulevard
Suite 232
Minneapolis, MN 55416
1-877-845-8392
www.picturewindowbooks.com

Printed in the United States of America.

Library of Congress Cataloging-in-Publication Data
Shea, Kitty.
Out and about at the supermarket / by Kitty Shea ; illustrated by Becky Shipe.
p. cm. — (Field trips)
Summary: Store employee Mark gives a guided tour of a supermarket, where he
explains such things as which are the most popular foods, why some foods must
be kept frozen, and how groceries should be packed in bags. Includes an activity
and other learning resources.
Includes bibliographical references and index.
ISBN 1-4048-0295-9 (Reinforced Library Binding)
1. Supermarkets—Juvenile literature. [1. Supermarkets.] I. Shipe, Becky, ill.
II. Title. III. Field trips (Picture Window Books)
HF5469 .S525 2004
381'.149—dc22
                                                    2003016157

We're going on a field trip to the supermarket.
We can't wait!

Things to find out:

Where does the supermarket get all
of its food?

How do you find what you're looking for
in a supermarket?

How does a cash register work?

How do you know what something costs
if it doesn't have a price sticker?

Hello, everyone! I'm Mark. I work here at the supermarket. Today we'll see how food gets to us, so we can get it to you. All day long, trucks deliver food and other goods to the supermarket. Some food comes right from farms. Other products come from companies that make and package them for us.

4

A forklift meets delivery trucks at the central loading dock. It helps unload the trucks. Cold or frozen foods go into big coolers. Other items go in the back room until there's space for them on the store shelves.

5

Here is Stephanie, one of our stock clerks. She puts cans, boxes, and cartons on the shelves. Prices are on the front of the shelves, right below the products. We want our shelves to look full and neat—never empty and messy. See how Stephanie turns all the products so the name on each one faces out?

Shelves are lined up in rows in the supermarket. Between each row is an aisle for walking. The sign above each aisle tells you what items you'll find in that aisle.

SOAPS CLEANERS

FRUITS & VEGETABLES

Milk, fruits, vegetables, and meat are called staples. These are foods that almost everyone buys. Supermarkets put staples around the edge of the store so shoppers can find them easily.

7

Fruits and vegetables are called produce. Look! The lettuce is getting a shower. We mist the produce with water so it stays crisp and fresh. You can pick your produce out of the bins yourself or buy it in packages. Some packaged produce has already been washed and cut for you.

Supermarkets sell more bananas and apples than any other fruits. The most popular vegetables are potatoes and lettuce.

Are hamburgers your favorite food? Do you eat turkey on Thanksgiving? You'll find beef, pork, turkey, chicken, and fish in our meat and seafood department. Everything is kept cold or frozen so it's safe to eat and tastes good when you cook it.

FREEZER

MEATS

Hamburgers are ground beef. The beef comes to us in big chunks. The butcher grinds the beef and divides it into portions that fit on trays. Then a machine weighs, wraps, and puts prices on the trays.

11

Dairy products come from cows. Milk, cheese, butter, and yogurt need to be refrigerated to keep them fresh. I like stocking the dairy case during the summer, because it is nice and cold. We work in the back room and slide the milk in from the back of the case.

Dairy products don't stay fresh for long. Milk turns sour if it isn't used in a certain amount of time. In the supermarket, each dairy product is stamped with a SELL BY date. If the item hasn't sold by that date, the supermarket has to throw it away.

Have you ever helped make orange juice for breakfast? The frozen foods department is where you'll find frozen juice. The freezers also hold vegetables, pizza, and much more. I'll bet you like ice cream! We carry lots of flavors. We put chocolate syrup and ice-cream cones next to the freezer. This gives shoppers ideas for yummy desserts.

Supermarkets have special displays for items that are on sale. Often the end of each row has a display with a big sign. If the display looks good, shoppers might stop and buy the item on sale.

Busy people often don't have time to cook and bake, so our deli and bakery help them out. We make salads and other dishes and bake breads in our kitchen here at the store.

DELI

HOT   HO

Everything is ready to take home and eat. Mmm. Smell the fresh bread!

Many supermarkets are extra busy between five and seven o'clock in the evening. Shoppers are picking up food to eat for dinner. Saturdays and Sundays are also busy times. That's when people fill their shopping carts with groceries for the week ahead.

I'm sure you've all been through a checkout lane. Every lane has a cashier and a cash register. A cash register is a computer, calculator, and bank—all in one. Some produce items need to be weighed to see how much they cost. Other items have bar codes instead of price stickers.

A bar code is a row of thin and fat lines. The cashier runs the bar code over a scanner. The scanner reads the code and tells the cash register how much the item costs.

19

At some stores, shoppers bag their own groceries. Our supermarket has people called packers who bag your groceries for you. Be ready to tell them if you want paper or plastic bags.

Packers put heavy things, such as cans, in the bottom of a grocery bag. Bread and eggs go on top so they won't get squished or broken. Frozen foods go together to help keep them cold for the trip home.

You must be hungry after seeing all this food! Here's a shiny red apple to eat. Come again soon!

GO SHOPPING FOR DINNER

What you need:

a sheet or pad of paper for your menu and shopping list
a pen or pencil
a menu (the one provided here or one you create yourself)
money to pay for your groceries

Menu

grilled cheese sandwiches
tomato soup
carrot and celery sticks
pear slices
chocolate chip cookies
milk

What you do:

1. Make sure you have an adult to help you.
2. Write down each menu item or draw a picture of it. You may use the menu above or create your own.
3. Decide what you will need for each menu item and write your grocery list. For example, you will need bread, butter, and cheese to make the grilled cheese sandwiches. Write down or draw these items.
4. Look in your kitchen to see if you already have any of the things on your grocery list. When you find an item, cross it off your list.
5. Ask an adult if there are any coupons for the foods on your list so you can save some money.
6. Go to the supermarket. When you find each item, check its price label on the shelf. Is there another item like it that costs less?
7. Once you have all the items on your list, take your shopping cart to a checkout lane. Give the cashier your coupons, if you have any. Watch as the items are scanned and the prices show up on the register screen. Pay the cashier the total amount.
8. Ask if you can bag your own groceries. Put heavy items on the bottom. Put the bread and cookies on top so they won't get squished.
9. Read your receipt. Did you get everything that was on your list?
10. Go home and unpack your grocery bags. Make and enjoy your meal!

FUN FACTS

- Piggly Wiggly opened the first self-service grocery store in the United States in 1916. The first U.S. supermarket was King Kullen Grocery Company in New York, which opened in 1930.

- A supermarket is a big grocery store. Many supermarkets have the same name because they are part of a group of big stores called a chain. Some smaller grocery stores are called mom-and-pop stores, because they are often run by families. Stores at gas stations are called convenience stores. They make it easy for people to buy quick snacks and basic foods such as bread and milk.

- The first item ever scanned in a supermarket was a pack of chewing gum in 1974.

- Cashiers make up the largest number of workers in a supermarket, followed by the clerks who stock the shelves. Other workers include butchers, bakers, deli cooks, people who hand out food samples, packers, cleaners, freight movers, and department and store managers.

- Fresh fruits, vegetables, and meats can be sold without a label. Everything else must have a label that tells what the product is, who made it, how much is inside, and what's in it. Food labels also include information such as how much fat and sugar a product has in it.

GLOSSARY

aisle (ILE)—a space to walk between rows. In a supermarket, the aisles are between rows of products on shelves.

cashier—a person who runs a cash register

cash register—the machine that adds up the price of groceries and has a drawer for money

coupon—a printed piece of paper that's good for a certain amount of money off the price of a product

deli—short for delicatessen, which is the area of the supermarket that sells cooked or prepared foods that are ready to eat

produce (PROH-dooss)—fresh fruits and vegetables

receipt—a piece of paper printed by the cash register that lists each item that was bought and its price

scanner—a machine that reads a package's bar code using a beam of light and then tells the cash register how much the item costs

staple—an important and basic food item that is eaten by most people

TO LEARN MORE

At the Library

Hill, Mary. *Signs at the Store*. New York: Children's Press, 2003.

Krull, Kathleen. *Supermarket*. New York: Holiday House, 2001.

Pluckrose, Henry. *In the Supermarket*. New York: Franklin Watts, 1998.

Saunders-Smith, Gail. *The Supermarket*. Mankato, Minn.: Pebble Books, 1998.

Schaefer, Lola M. *Supermarket*. Chicago: Heinemann Library, 2000.

On the Web

Fact Hound offers a safe, fun way to find Web sites related to this book. All of the sites on Fact Hound have been researched by our staff. *http://www.facthound.com*

1. Visit the Fact Hound home page.
2. Enter a search word related to this book, or type in this special code: 1404802959.
3. Click on the FETCH IT button.

Your trusty Fact Hound will fetch the best sites for you!

INDEX

DATE DUE			

090504684

381
SHE

Shea, Kitty.

Out and about at the
supermarket

STONELEIGH ELEMENTARY SCHOOL
BALTIMORE CO. PUBLIC SCHOOLS
CD 2006